POSITIVE AFFIRMATIONS AND ACTIONS FOR
Self Love

LEARN TO LOVE YOURSELF, CREATE HAPPINESS, IMPROVE YOUR CONFIDENCE & BUILD INNER STRENGTH

🐢 Turtle Publishing

Published by Turtle Publishing
All rights reserved.

Printed on demand in Australia, United States and United Kingdom.

Written & designed by Kathy Shanks
© Kathy Shanks 2021
Illustrations by Freepik Storyset & Turtle Publishing

No part of this publication may be reproduced, stored in a retrieval system, or transmitted in any form or by any means, electronic, mechanical, photocopying, recording or otherwise, without the prior written permission of the author.

Under no circumstances will any blame or legal responsibility be held against the publisher, or author, for any damages, reparation, or monetary loss due to the information contained within this book including, but not limited to — errors, omissions, or inaccuracies. Either directly or indirectly. You are responsible for your own choices, actions, and results.

Legal Notice: This book is copyright protected. This book is only for personal use. You cannot amend, distribute, sell, use, quote or paraphrase any part, or the content within this book, without the consent of the author or publisher.

Disclaimer: Please note the information contained within this document is for educational and entertainment purposes only. All effort has been executed to present accurate, up to date, and reliable, complete information. No warranties of any kind are declared or implied. Readers acknowledge that the author is not engaging in the rendering of legal, financial, medical or professional advice. The content within this book has been derived from various sources. Please consult a licensed professional before attempting any techniques outlined in this book.

SPECIAL BONUS
FREE BOOKS

FREE Workbook to begin an intentional journaling practice.

FREE 30 Days to Greater Self Love Program

Get FREE unlimited access to these AND all of my new books by joining our fan base!

SCAN WITH YOUR CAMERA OR GO TO
bit.ly/AffGifts

How to use this book

On the left-hand pages are affirmations. On the right-hand pages are actions for you to take towards strengthening your self-love.

You may like to work through this book one page per day, or perhaps you'd like to trust divine guidance. Hold this book close to your heart or navel, close your eyes, take three gentle breaths, and as you breathe out on the third breath, open the book. We trust that you will be guided to the page you need the most.

Introduction

One of the first things we learn as a child is to love others. Growing up, we're constantly reminded to be kind and helpful to the people around us. It's no surprise that somewhere along the way, many of us learn that selflessness is a prized virtue and that putting ourselves and our own needs before others is selfish—something to be avoided at all costs.

Now, there's absolutely nothing wrong with treating others with love and kindness—there can never be enough of it in the world! But, to be a light in someone else's life, you've got to *kindle your own spark first*. Everything starts with loving yourself.

Self-love is such a powerful force. Not only does your capacity to care for others grow as you care for yourself, but so does your overall wellbeing. Whether you notice it or not, constantly putting yourself last on your list of priorities and pushing your own needs to the bottom of the pile takes a considerable toll on your happiness. If you're feeling tired, drained, or overwhelmed, perhaps it's time to give yourself the love and care *you* undoubtedly deserve.

Self-love is much more than a feeling or a mere state of being. It's a *commitment* to tend to your own needs and do things to fill your cup. It means actively being compassionate towards yourself, accepting who you are, and celebrating your authentic self… flaws and all.

In a world where we're wired to chase relentlessly after success—*whatever* our vision of that is—cultivating self-love can definitely be tough. We tend to be hardest on ourselves, struggling under the pressure to become our best selves and measuring our own worth against where we are in relation to our goals.

Here's the thing, though: self-love is unconditional.

We are already worthy, wherever we are in our respective journeys. We are all *enough*. Self-love shouldn't have to wait until you land your dream job, achieve the 'perfect' body, or make the 'right' connections. True self-love meets you where you're at, *just as you are*.

It's important to recognise that loving yourself doesn't just happen overnight. It's a journey in itself—a dynamic process of unlearning negative, limiting beliefs and behaviour and replacing these with a healthy self-care practice.

This could mean different things to different people. Everyone expresses and receives love differently, and self-love is no exception.

No matter what your own personal path looks like, though, affirmations can be extremely valuable along the way.

Thought patterns are rooted in actual connections in the brain—repeatedly thinking something strengthens its specific pathway and triggers a chemical response that makes it easier to default to later on. This simply means that words hold power, and affirmations can be a great way to harness this.

The very act of repeating affirmations to yourself allows you to explore a reflective, meditative state. This alone can calm the mind, helping relieve any anxiety and the stress of day to day life.

As consistent self-affirmation practice reinforces your sense of self and allows you to identify what you truly value in life, it can also be an amazing way to boost your confidence and build a foundation of self-belief.

Finally, and perhaps most importantly, affirmations can also help you find joy in both the person you are, and who you are still striving to be. Positive self-talk *unlocks* a deep sense of contentment and happiness from within. At the same time, it keeps you motivated and empowers you to focus your energy and send it towards your goals.

By setting aside time each day for some positive self-talk or simply keeping a couple of affirmations in your back pocket to call to mind whenever you need them, you can take control of your wellbeing and drive your own narrative.

It doesn't have to be fancy—you can choose to say the statements out loud, write the ones that resonate with you the most in your journal, or just close your eyes and focus on the words quietly.

Combined with conscious, mindful (and fun!) self-care activities and exercises, repeating these powerful statements to yourself regularly creates new, healthy patterns—ones that allow you to nourish your mind, body, heart, and soul.

"Demonstrate love by giving it, unconditionally, to yourself. And as you do, you will attract others into your life who will love you without conditions."

- Paul Ferrini

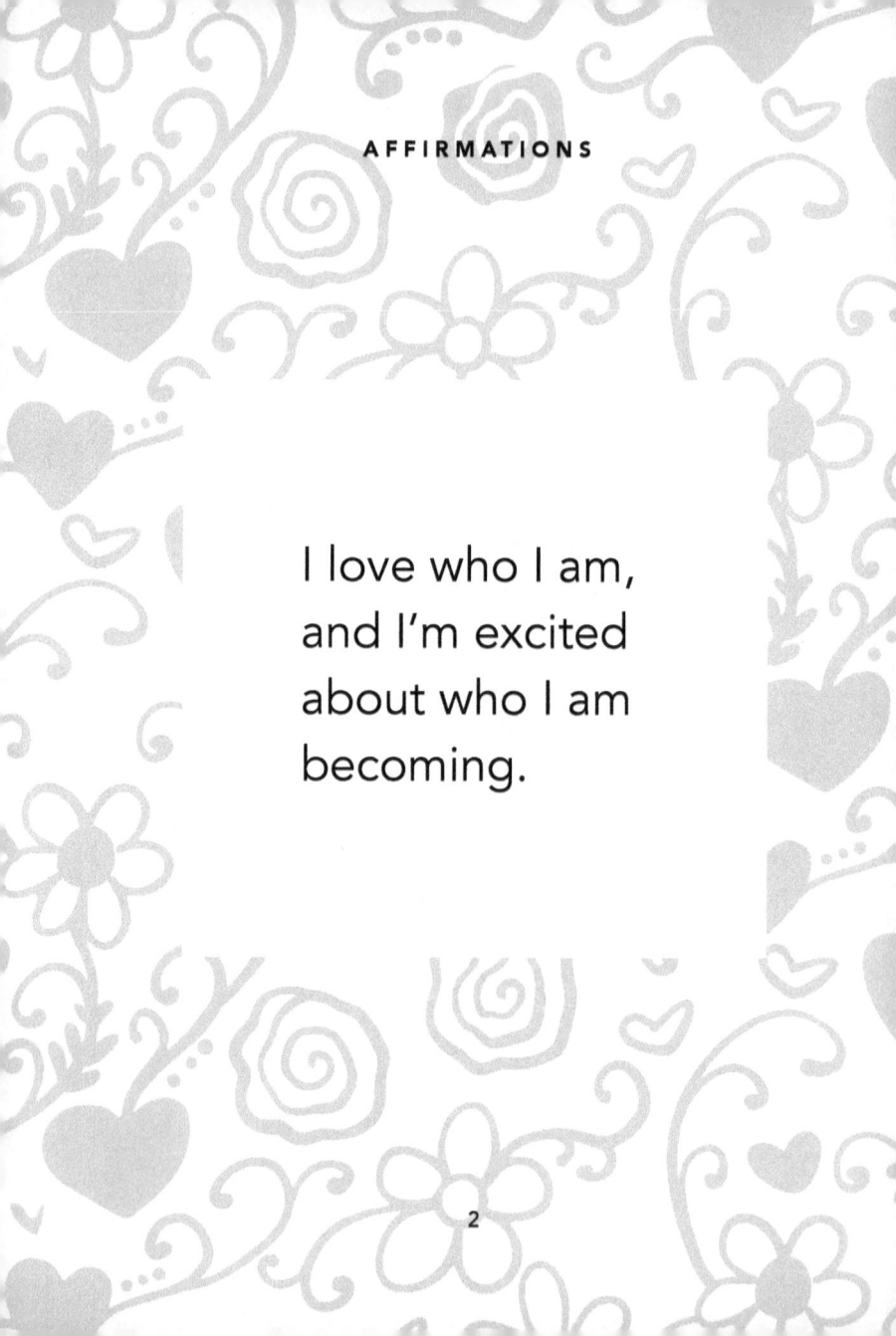

AFFIRMATIONS

I love who I am, and I'm excited about who I am becoming.

ACTIONS

Pick some affirmations that really resonate with you, and practice saying these out loud to yourself in front of the mirror each day.

AFFIRMATIONS

My thoughts and feelings matter.

ACTIONS

Once a week, treat yourself to something you really, truly enjoy.

AFFIRMATIONS

I am worthy of love and affection.

ACTIONS

Run a luxurious bath with your favourite scent and give yourself as much time as you want to enjoy it.

AFFIRMATIONS

I accept myself wholly, flaws and all.

ACTIONS

List down 10 things you are proud of about your character and who you are.

AFFIRMATIONS

I am happy to
be uniquely me.

ACTIONS

List down 10 things you adore about your body.

AFFIRMATIONS

I deserve to
spend time
and energy
on things that
make me happy.

ACTIONS

Create a bedtime ritual that helps you wind down and relax. It doesn't have to take long or be complicated—it can be as simple as having a cup of tea or listening to a soothing song.

AFFIRMATIONS

My needs are important and deserve attention.

ACTIONS

Put on some of your favourite upbeat music, turn it up, and dance!

AFFIRMATIONS

I am deeply committed to caring for myself.

ACTIONS

It's time to finally get rid of those clothes in the depths of your closet that no longer fit.

AFFIRMATIONS

I am capable of setting healthy boundaries for myself.

ACTIONS

Time for a social media audit—unfollow any accounts or influencers that make you feel bad about yourself or don't add any value to your life.

AFFIRMATIONS

I am allowed to put myself first.

ACTIONS

Make moisturising a post-shower habit—give yourself a little massage while you're at it!

AFFIRMATIONS

I am wonderful and special.

ACTIONS

Re-read your favourite childhood book.

AFFIRMATIONS

I deserve rest
whenever I
need it.

ACTIONS

Spend a rainy or chilly day curled up with a mug of your favourite hot beverage and a good book.

AFFIRMATIONS

I deserve the space that I occupy in this world.

ACTIONS

Create a personal nook for yourself at home. It can be as simple as setting a comfortable chair by a window and adding your favourite blanket or pillow.

AFFIRMATIONS

I accept and love my imperfections because they are part of what makes me who I am.

ACTIONS

Write down the best compliment you've ever received.

AFFIRMATIONS

I have the
power to lift
myself up.

ACTIONS

Try a new hairstyle or fashion trend you've had your eye on for a while.

AFFIRMATIONS

I honour my inner power.

ACTIONS

Go out for a meal by yourself and focus on enjoying your own company.

AFFIRMATIONS

Every part of me is worthy of respect.

ACTIONS

Start a daily mood tracker on your phone or in your journal.

AFFIRMATIONS

I am allowed to be proud of my accomplishments and celebrate these.

ACTIONS

Try to revive an old hobby or interest that you were forced to drop for whatever reason.

AFFIRMATIONS

I create my own journey and my own story.

ACTIONS

Put on your favourite party outfit (you know, the one you don't get enough opportunities to wear) to lounge around at home.

AFFIRMATIONS

I am filled with
light and grace.

ACTIONS

Do an at-home spa day with a DIY face or hair mask.

AFFIRMATIONS

I am both infinitely loved and loving.

ACTIONS

Find and learn a breathing exercise that works for you, and use it whenever you need a little pocket of calm in your day.

AFFIRMATIONS

I let go of thoughts that do not serve me.

ACTIONS

Can you go an entire day without checking social media? Try it out and see how it makes you feel.

AFFIRMATIONS

I allow all negativity, pain, or anxiety to fall away from me.

ACTIONS

Allow yourself to fall down a rabbit hole of funny or cute videos online for a bit.

AFFIRMATIONS

With every breath, I welcome in love, light, and happiness.

ACTIONS

Start that book that you've been meaning to get around to.

AFFIRMATIONS

I release any expectations I feel pressured to live up to.

ACTIONS

List down 5 things you're capable of that not many people can do.

AFFIRMATIONS

I am a child of the universe.

ACTIONS

How long has it been since you've walked barefoot outdoors, on the grass or at the beach?

AFFIRMATIONS

I am proud to
be a work in
progress.

ACTIONS

Designate one day a month where you have absolutely nothing planned. Feel free to spend that day lazing about or just going with the flow.

AFFIRMATIONS

I am fully capable of standing on my own two feet.

ACTIONS

If you have a junk drawer or a specific long-standing pile of clutter in your house, now's the time to get around to organising it finally.

AFFIRMATIONS

I am a beautiful person inside and out.

ACTIONS

Re-read your old journals or posts just to appreciate how far you've come.

AFFIRMATIONS

I deserve all the happiness in the world.

ACTIONS

Make time to hang out with a friend who's fun to be around.

AFFIRMATIONS

I love my body, including its flaws and imperfections.

ACTIONS

Take a makeup-free, filterless selfie and find 5 things you love about it.

AFFIRMATIONS

I am enough, always and in all ways.

ACTIONS

Plan a day trip or vacation—it doesn't matter if it's happening soon or if you even end up going or not. Just have fun with dreaming it all up!

AFFIRMATIONS

I am filled
with grit and
determination.

ACTIONS

What makes you feel like your best self? List down everything you can think of.

AFFIRMATIONS

I rise to every challenge in my own unique way.

ACTIONS

On your next grocery trip, pick up one fun food item you wouldn't normally buy.

AFFIRMATIONS

I am more
than my past
mistakes.

ACTIONS

Sleep in on a weekend morning!

AFFIRMATIONS

I am proud to
be my own
cheerleader.

ACTIONS

Listen to your favourite album from start to finish.

AFFIRMATIONS

I am in control of my own happiness.

ACTIONS

As part of your nighttime routine, take time to gently and thoroughly cleanse your face and 'take the day off.'

AFFIRMATIONS

Fear cannot
stand in my way.

ACTIONS

List down 5 healthy boundaries or non-negotiables that you would like to start enforcing.

AFFIRMATIONS

I am alive and flourishing.

ACTIONS

You don't need a reason to buy yourself flowers!

AFFIRMATIONS

I am a one-of-a-kind work of art.

ACTIONS

Turn your afternoon coffee into a treat with a cinnamon stick, a sprinkle of cocoa powder, or a dollop of whipped cream.

AFFIRMATIONS

I sow seeds of love in the darkest parts of myself.

ACTIONS

Give your room or any personal space a makeover. Rearrange your furniture, paint an accent wall, or just hang up some colourful new curtains—it's all up to you, and it doesn't have to be anything major.

AFFIRMATIONS

The light of my soul amazes me.

ACTIONS

Listen to an uplifting, motivating song. Close your eyes, and enjoy how the music makes you feel.

AFFIRMATIONS

I exude beauty and grace.

ACTIONS

The next time you eat out, give yourself permission to order that dessert.

AFFIRMATIONS

Confidence comes naturally to me.

ACTIONS

Belt out your favourite tunes!

AFFIRMATIONS

There is nobody
else in this
world exactly
like me.

ACTIONS

Re-watch a favourite movie or episode of a series.

AFFIRMATIONS

My heart is strong and proud.

ACTIONS

Describe your superpower.

AFFIRMATIONS

I tap into a
deep awareness
of who I am.

ACTIONS

Ask for a big hug from someone who gives you comfort.

AFFIRMATIONS

I listen closely
to the song of
my soul.

ACTIONS

When you're feeling stressed or anxious, let it all go on paper—list down everything that's weighing on your mind.

AFFIRMATIONS

Loving energy surrounds me.

ACTIONS

Write about feeling beautiful in your own skin, whether it's a moment you've experienced or just how that might feel regularly.

AFFIRMATIONS

I am safe in
the universe's
embrace.

ACTIONS

Set aside a few minutes each day to simply get lost in your own thoughts—you can even set an actual timer or alarm if that works for you.

AFFIRMATIONS

I am perfectly imperfect.

ACTIONS

Practice always receiving compliments openly and graciously. Even when you feel you don't deserve them, accept them with a bright smile and a sincere 'thank you!'

AFFIRMATIONS

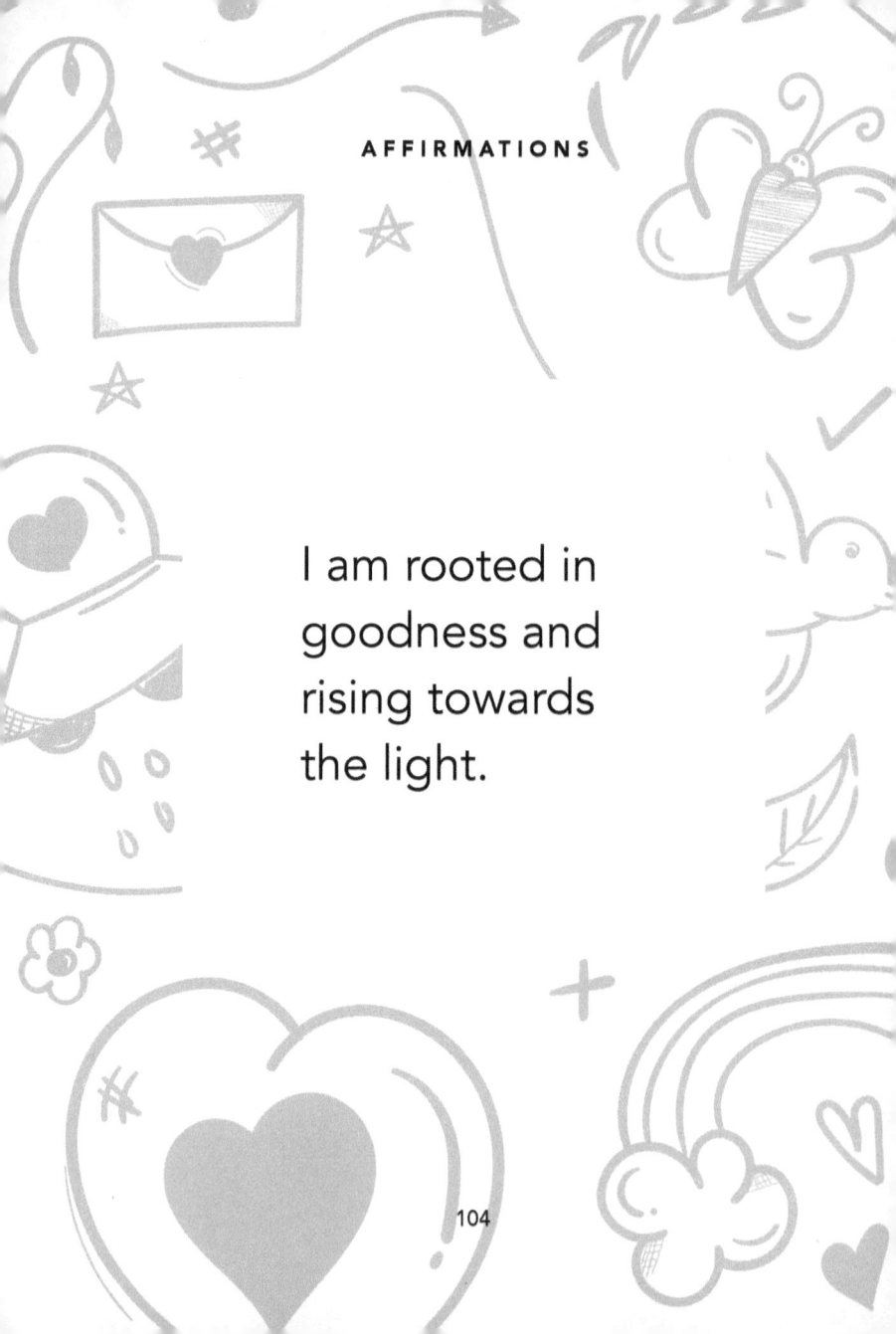

I am rooted in goodness and rising towards the light.

ACTIONS

If possible, open all your windows and curtains to let fresh air in.

AFFIRMATIONS

The loudest
voice in my life
is my own.

ACTIONS

What do you feel you need more of in your life? What's stopping you from getting or having that?

AFFIRMATIONS

I am at peace with the past, present, and future.

ACTIONS

Re-evaluate your relationships. Ask yourself if it might be time to let go of or stop investing emotionally in those that bring toxicity and negativity into your life.

AFFIRMATIONS

I am capable of so much more than I ever dreamed.

ACTIONS

Make a 'happy jar' by writing down little treats for yourself on slips of paper, mixing up tangible things like "have a chocolate bar" with activities like "phone your favourite person." Every time you need a dose of positivity, pick something out of the jar.

AFFIRMATIONS

My soul always
finds its way.

ACTIONS

The next time a negative thought about yourself pops into your head, imagine saying it to or about someone you love. Chances are, you'll be able to turn that thought right around.

AFFIRMATIONS

Negative energy has no place in my life.

ACTIONS

Get down on the floor to just play and roll around with your pet.

AFFIRMATIONS

Joy begins
within me.

ACTIONS

List down 3 things you'd like to forgive yourself for… and try to work on following through.

AFFIRMATIONS

I am allowed to
move and grow
at my own pace.

ACTIONS

Give yourself permission to say 'no' to something.

AFFIRMATIONS

I express myself confidently with pride and joy.

ACTIONS

Paint your fingernails and toenails a bright, happy colour you've always wanted to try.

AFFIRMATIONS

I respect myself deeply and completely.

ACTIONS

Treat yourself to new bedsheets.

AFFIRMATIONS

I love myself unconditionally.

ACTIONS

When you least feel like it, take a deep breath and put on the biggest smile you can muster—it won't be long until you begin to feel your mood lift as well.

AFFIRMATIONS

I am worthy
of the utmost
care and
compassion.

ACTIONS

Wash and deep condition your hair.

AFFIRMATIONS

My capacity to love grows each day.

ACTIONS

Every day, make it a point to do one good thing for your mind, body, and heart.

AFFIRMATIONS

I honour my
unique journey.

ACTIONS

Make a creative collage, illustration, or even just a written list of all your favourite things. What's your favourite movie? Colour? Season? Place? Food? What else can you think of that makes you the absolute happiest?

AFFIRMATIONS

Loving myself is
a process.

ACTIONS

Look up an interesting cocktail (or mocktail) and make yourself one to enjoy after a long workday.

AFFIRMATIONS

I protect the unique spark within.

ACTIONS

Write down 3 things you don't like about yourself. Then, rewrite them into positive, affirming statements.

AFFIRMATIONS

I am always changing for the better.

ACTIONS

Grab yourself a healthy, energising mid-afternoon snack.

AFFIRMATIONS

I release anger to make room for love.

ACTIONS

Remember that needing support isn't a weakness—reach out for help whenever you need it.

AFFIRMATIONS

I am fuelled by love and filled with joy.

ACTIONS

Doodle without worrying about it looking good or turning out well.

AFFIRMATIONS

This wonderful path of mine is unlike any other.

ACTIONS

Learn about your love language.

AFFIRMATIONS

I am braver than
I could have
ever imagined.

ACTIONS

Go on a relaxing drive through your favourite neighbourhood.

AFFIRMATIONS

I stand by my truth, always.

ACTIONS

Make yourself a full-course meal at home.

AFFIRMATIONS

I trust my
wisdom and
honour my
intuition.

ACTIONS

Try not to scroll through your phone in bed, whether first thing in the morning or while waiting to fall asleep.

AFFIRMATIONS

I free myself
from every
doubt and fear.

ACTIONS

After a long day, take your time and be mindful about how it feels to change out of your work outfit and into your favourite comfortable clothes.

Also available by **Kathy Shanks**...

Guided Journaling is available worldwide as print or ebook at Amazon, Booktopia, Barnes & Noble and all good bookstores.

Also available in Australia from **turtlepublishing.com.au**

Inside this book you'll discover how to use my method of journaling to:

- Work towards creating balance for heart, mind, body and soul without sacrificing career and relationships
- Create rituals that help you develop gratitude
- Use daily affirmations to practice positivity and manifest your future dreams
- Discover strategies to improve your relationships, build your life mission, start a side hustle, discover yourself, develop self-love, improve your health AND improve your mindset

It seems too good to be true, right! Organising your thoughts and dreams in 10-20 minutes a day can be that one simple change that actually makes your dreams become a reality.

Make your journal your safe haven, a place of nurturing for you to come and reflect, clear your mind, set goals, develop gratitude, make plans, dream, and take steps towards the future that has always seemed just out of reach.

Please join our journaling community at
facebook.com/groups/kathyshanks
for exclusive insider access to updates and releases

Also available in the
Guided Journaling Series...

Journaling for a
Balanced Life with a
Health focus

Journaling for a
Balanced Life with a
Life Mission focus

Journaling for a
Balanced Life with a
focus on the **Heart**

Journaling for a
Balanced Life with a
Gratitude & **Manifest** focus

We have a selection of *journals* available worldwide as
print or ebook at Amazon, Booktopia,
Barnes & Noble and all good bookstores.
Also available in Australia from **turtlepublishing.com.au**

www.ingramcontent.com/pod-product-compliance
Lightning Source LLC
Chambersburg PA
CBHW020323010526
44107CB00054B/1957